# Can I Play Too?

# Can I Play Too?

Physical Education for Physically Disabled Children
in Mainstream Schools

### Sheila E. Jowsey

## David Fulton Publishers
### London

David Fulton Publishers Ltd
2 Barbon Close, London WC1N 3JX

First published in Great Britain by
David Fulton Publishers, 1992

Note: The right of the author to be identified as the author of this work has been asserted by her in accordance with the Copyright, Designs and Patents Act 1988.

*British Library of Cataloguing in Publication Data*

A catalogue record for this book is available from the British Library

ISBN 1-85346-217-9

Typeset by Chapterhouse, Formby L37 3PX
Printed in Great Britain by Bell and Bain Ltd., Glasgow.

# Contents

# List of Figures

# List of Illustrations

# Acknowledgements

I would like to thank all the staff and pupils, past and present, at Kingsley Special School, Kettering, and the many children in mainstream schools whom I have met through my work at Kingsley – without them this book would not have been possible.

Thanks, also, are due to Paul Smith of Rothwell, for producing the photographs, and to the staff of Kettering Professional Development Centre for their patience in the preparation of the typescript.

Finally, I am particularly grateful to my parents, and to those friends who have been involved with the book from its conception, whose continued interest, advice, support and patience have encouraged me to bring it at last to completion.

# Foreword

Over the last decade or so the number of pupils with special educational needs, including physical disabilities, in mainstream schools has increased considerably. Physical Education (PE) is essentially concerned with movement and consequently any pupil with a physical or sensory impairment, or a motor disability is likely to have special needs in this area of the curriculum regardless of whether he or she is recognised as having special needs in other academic subjects.

Most PE teachers would claim that they have always taught mixed ability classes. However, the integration of pupils with physical disabilities can present real problems to many teachers; all too often these pupils either take no active part in lessons or are expected to cope as best they can regardless of the appropriateness of the activity.

The reasons for this can be several and varied but generally teachers lack the information they need about the implications of impairment (a term covering a wide range of diagnosed conditions) and, for example, whether the condition is likely to improve, deteriorate, change or remain static. Uppermost in the mind of many teachers is a concern for safety, uncertainty about attainment levels, or a lack of knowledge about how to adapt equipment or modify tasks.

All teachers need to know the implications of particular impairments for motor control and co-ordination, muscular strength, endurance, mobility, flexibility and spatial awareness. They also need to know which physical activities and sports are appropriate, as well as how they can be modified for individuals and groups. Participation in athletics, for example, may require wheels to be substituted for legs in track events. The sense of involvement and competition that is generated is no less valid.

This book is a valuable resource for teachers planning lessons and extra-curricular activities for pupils with disabilities. It contains a wealth of information on the implications for participation presented by particular impairments and should give teachers the confidence to select and present tasks that are appropriate, stimulating and challenging.

For all pupils the aims of PE should be the same. All have entitlement to a broad and balanced programme including the six areas of activity identified in the PE National Curriculum. Yes, 'you can play too', even if in certain contexts special provision outside the mainstream PE curriculum is necessary to ensure that both breadth and balance are provided.

Sally H Johns
April, 1992
[Formerly H.M. Inspector of Schools]

# Preface

Physically disabled children in mainstream schools can find integration ends at the gym door (Fisher, 1988, p. 6)

yet

for children who are physically handicapped, the benefits which can accrue from a programme of physical education are immense (Price, 1980, p. 5).

This book is an attempt to equip teachers with the information and practical advice needed in order for them to feel confident in opening wide the gym door to all disabled youngsters whom they meet. It aims to enable them to provide the varied and challenging PE programme which is the children's need and entitlement and to fully address the demands of the National Curriculum. It is written by a PE teacher who has had many years experience of teaching the subject, to children of all ages in both ordinary and special schools and who has also had the chance to gain much from the expertise of others.

## References

Fisher, A. (1988) 'Just one of the boys', *Times Educational Supplement*, 3778, 25.

Price, A. (1980) *Physical Education and the Physically Handicapped Child*, London: Lepus.

# Introduction

Lisa is a teenager with brittle bones. She has normal intelligence, but her condition has caused considerable deformity; she is constantly wheelchair-bound, often with a fractured long bone to contend with, too. A deteriorating muscle condition means that David's movements are becoming progressively weaker and more laboured and his mobility is now seriously impaired, but he is determined to get about his junior school without resorting to using his wheelchair, whenever possible. Steve's condition, caused by damage to his brain when he was born, means that he has muscle weakness and spasm in the limbs on one side of his body and a squint. As a consequence he walks with a limp and avoids using his affected arm. Spina bifida is the reason for Paul's unsteady gait, incontinence and perceptual problems, but he is slowly learning to cope with all the demands of a busy infant classroom and with his own physical management.

With the growing move towards integration which has taken place during the last decade, Lisa, David, Steve and Paul all now attend their local mainstream schools. Since 1981, Local Education Authorities have, of course, had a duty to educate all children with special needs in ordinary schools, wherever it is feasible to do so. They are also responsible for making better provision for those children with less obvious, less severe difficulties who have always formed a significant proportion of our mainstream school population.

All teachers, therefore, are now teachers of children with special educational needs. But we know that many feel ill-prepared to meet this new challenge, particularly where physically disabled pupils are involved, because of uncertainty about managing the condition itself. In practical subjects the task of providing a broad and balanced curriculum appropriate for the wide range of children like those to whom we have been introduced, each with their own very special individual needs, can be especially daunting and one which is sometimes avoided. Too often, it seems, physically disabled youngsters in mainstream schools do not receive the PE they need and deserve. Yet their need is probably even greater than that of their able-bodied peers. Physical activity, in the first instance, is important as a means of gaining and maintaining health and fitness. It should also give the children opportunity to learn how to function in a physical environment and to manage their bodies appropriately – both of which are essential skills, then to experience enjoyment, success and all the other physical, social and psychological benefits of the activity.

The National Curriculum (NC) document (August, 1991) makes some basic recommendations about the way programmes of study can be applied to certain groups of children with special educational needs, and so proposes that no child should be excluded from NC PE. Furthermore, it strongly advocates participation alongside able-bodied peers, wherever this is possible. However, I appreciate that many teachers feel they have neither sufficient knowledge about various disabilities, nor information about how to differentiate their subject, even using these recommendations, to cater adequately for atypical children in their normal teaching groups.

This book, therefore, attempts to remedy that situation and to overcome teachers' natural apprehensions about managing PE, which for many are heightened now that we have the introduction of the NC for PE. The underlying philosophy behind it is one of facilitation, of enabling staff to make accessible what is the children's need and entitlement, without attempting to dictate conditions, organization or content. 'Entitlement' and 'access' are, of course, two of the major principles which the NC Working Party (1991) suggests should underpin any PE programme for children with special educational needs.

The book provides basic information, practical tips and suggestions for alternative strategies. It is not intended as a PE syllabus, as lesson material, nor as a comprehensive text on physical disability: these areas have been fully documented elsewhere (see Appendix B). Rather, it is hoped that by being presented as a practical resource or handbook, it will bridge the gap between the two disciplines of education and therapy, and so help teachers of youngsters like Lisa and David, Paul and Steve, to fully appreciate the dimensions of their curriculum area, and the needs of their pupils for, 'in this situation more than in any other, the teacher needs to know his subject and his subjects' (Price, 1980, p. 5).

There are no categorically right or wrong ways for teachers to match subject to subjects, nor simple, straightforward solutions to answer all eventualities. Nor should we expect there to be when every child and teacher, their own ability and experience and every learning/teaching environment is different. And, of course, it must be appreciated that each individual's needs are totally unique and can in no way be categorized by a label alone. Also, we must remember that at secondary level children are usually taught by subject specialists, whereas in the primary phase classteachers with general training are invariably responsible for PE too: some are far less confident than others regarding teaching the subject itself, without any extra facets to consider.

So there is no single blueprint, no master plan on teaching PE to special needs children in a mainstream environment, which could possibly advise teachers about every conceivable situation likely to be encountered. It would be presumptuous and restrictive to think that it might do so. Therefore, the aim here is to provide sufficient guidance through the information, advice, strategies and practical suggestions contained, to allow every teacher, whatever age-group they teach, whatever their own training and enthusiasm for the subject, to plan sufficiently flexibly and to teach with understanding and commitment.

Appropriate PE should then be fully accessible to all children and tailored to meet a whole host of very different, very individual special physical needs, in each unique situation.

## References

DES and Welsh Office (1991) *Physical Education for Ages 5-16*, Proposals of the Secretary of State for Education and Science and Secretary of State for Wales, London: HMSO.

Price, R. (1980) *Physical Education and the Physically Handicapped Child*, London: Lepus Books.

# Chapter 1

# The Value of Physical Education

As one of the NC foundation subjects, PE should now have a significant place on any school's timetable. In addition to improvements in the child's physical skills and well-being, the critical contribution that it can make to his or her development in social, psychological and academic areas is becoming more widely recognized and accepted. For young children in particular it is probably this subject, more than any other in the NC, which has the potential for more greatly influencing progress in other areas of learning and therefore for having the most far-reaching benefits.

There can be few people, nowadays, who question the value of PE and no further argument should be needed here to establish the benefits of PE for children of any age or aptitude. I am strongly convinced that PE can be even *more* beneficial to children with special physical needs; that access to an appropriately stimulating, challenging and enjoyable curriculum is their right and their entré to further development, and that we, as their teachers, must make every effort to meet that entitlement.

Young able-bodied children learn through exploration of their environment: they 'move to learn'. Their playful activities enable them to learn about themselves and about their relationships with others – play is the most natural medium for developing gross motor skills, and for learning to interact with others. As they grow older, games and sports provide the most powerful and most effective medium for socialization with their peers.

Disabled children invariably lack basic mobility to some degree; they are sometimes also overprotected or need to be immobilized or hospitalized for long periods. As a consequence, opportunities for exploring, for learning about how they can move around their surroundings, for playing alone or with others, can be severely limited. Experiences through which body and spatial awareness are developed are often restricted or not available, so that the original, physical difficulty may well become compounded. Older children can feel awkward, afraid or embarrassed and so avoid the very activity which is necessary to maintain even a basic level of health, fitness and mobility. They are far less likely, also, to be active out of school either through attendance at clubs or with the uniformed organizations, or informally, in play with their friends. So opportunity for socialization is often limited too.

PE, therefore, is an area of practical activity and experience which is vital to the growth and development of all children, but even more so in the case of children with physical disabilities. They need *more*, not less PE than their peers, so that they are able to keep fit and healthy, and are enabled to both 'learn to move' and 'move to learn', thus allowing all the benefits of the PE programme to accrue.

PE also provides a wonderful opportunity for developing the self-image and raising self-esteem and could be one significant area where these pupils can make choices, face challenges and experience real achievement. Furthermore, the considerable advantages of the 'hidden curriculum' implicit in the self-discovery, teamwork, problem-solving and discipline involved in the subject will then be available to them.

# Chapter 2

# The Aims of Physical Education

PE for all children, whatever their ability, focuses on a number of aims which are summarized in various forms in most PE texts. I have extended my general list of aims to include those which are particularly important, or of specific relevance, to physically disabled children. These reinforce my claims that this subject, probably more than any other, holds more potential opportunities and benefits for disabled youngsters than for their able-bodied classmates, and so should be made fully accessible to them.

I am convinced that we should aim, above all else, to provide for a sense of achievement. This can so often be lacking in the life of a disabled child, yet we all need to experience success in some form or other. Achievement in a physical activity can be immensely rewarding, beneficial and motivating to the child – an experience which, therefore, should not be denied him or her.

## General aims of the PE curriculum – applicable to *all* children

- To provide opportunity for success and achievement, so generating a positive feeling about physical activity, and motivating the child to attempt more.
- To optimize physical development, growth and fitness and foster a sense of well-being.
- To improve motor skills, develop body and spatial awareness and enhance the body image.
- To provide opportunity for social development through learning to cooperate with others and to function as a member of a group.
- To enable each child to express ideas and feelings through movement.
- To develop aesthetic awareness and foster creativity.
- To develop recreational and leisure-time pursuits.
- To provide opportunity for problem-solving and decision-making and for experiencing the success and failure of competition.
- To reinforce and develop current work in other curriculum areas through cross-curricular links or themes.

Through P.E dance it is always a creative aspect, not the race to the best.

## Additional specific aims for physically disabled children

- To develop particular skills as the individual begins to show readiness to do so, e.g. walking, or because they are needed to improve daily functioning, e.g. arm or grip strength.
- To help individuals to make the most of their abilities, whilst learning to compensate for their limitations and to gain a realistic perspective of their ability.
- To develop self-help skills, e.g. dressing and wheelchair transfers, so increasing competence in daily living situations and improving independence.
- To develop personal responsibility for physical control and management.
- To ensure that adequate and appropriate language stimulation and sensori-motor experiences are provided according to individual needs and to use the practical opportunities created to teach or reinforce language and concept development.
- To extend mobility, dexterity and independence in all children, through tasks which have functional bases and mastery of which achieves meaningful and worthwhile goals, with some purpose.

Although considerable emphasis is placed on the teaching of specific skills, safety procedures and self-care activities, none should of course be taught in isolation. Rather, they should be focused on as the situation arises within the lesson so that their relevance and importance are easily appreciated, for example, undressing practice becomes much more meaningful when it directly precedes a swimming lesson.

## How to meet these aims?

Few 'special' children will be able to follow a conventional PE programme without some adaptation of approach, objectives, equipment or pace. All, though, have the right to experience as wide a range of activities as that made available to their able-bodied peers. An 'extended' role is, therefore, clearly required of their teachers, a broader, deeper one which, on the one hand, necessitates close liaison with other professionals, in preparation, and on the other, attention being paid to a whole range of alternative approaches, strategies or activities, in order to make available as varied a curriculum as possible.

I have attempted to illustrate these points diagrammatically in Figure 1. The various traditional and alternative activities are discussed in detail in Chapter 4.

Considerable effort, adaptability and ingenuity will be required from teachers of atypical children like Lisa, Steve, David and Paul. Your task becomes more challenging, time-consuming and demanding – but do not be deterred: I firmly believe that ultimately it will be considerably more rewarding, more worthwhile and more satisfying to adults and children alike. A positive attitude, with high expectations, is essential if these children are to be appropriately challenged and extended.

**Figure 1** The dimensions of PE for children who have a physical disability

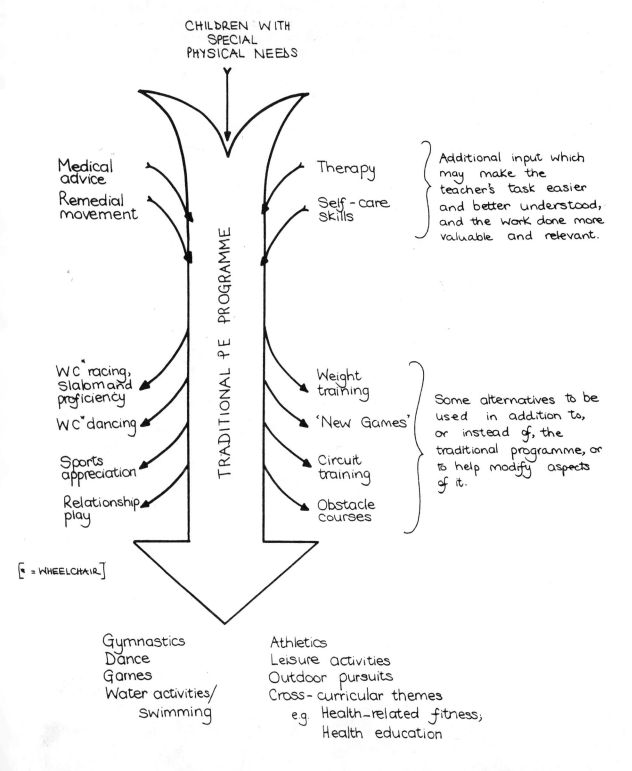

CHILDREN WITH
SPECIAL
PHYSICAL NEEDS

Medical advice

Remedial movement

Therapy

Self-care skills

Additional input which may make the teacher's task easier and better understood, and the work done more valuable and relevant.

TRADITIONAL PE PROGRAMME

WC* racing, slalom and proficiency

WC* dancing

Sports appreciation

Relationship play

Weight training

'New Games'

Circuit training

Obstacle courses

Some alternatives to be used in addition to, or instead of, the traditional programme, or to help modify aspects of it.

[* = WHEELCHAIR]

Gymnastics
Dance
Games
Water activities/ swimming

Athletics
Leisure activities
Outdoor pursuits
Cross-curricular themes
e.g. Health-related fitness;
Health education

The personal attributes needed to succeed with integrated classes are open attitudes, a determination to overcome difficulties and the ability to be innovative. There is also a need to remain aware of the realities of the environment, and the available facilities. A closed mind will inevitably fail, an open mind will find ways of succeeding! (BAALPE, 1989, p. 13).

## Reference

British Association of Advisers and Lecturers in Physical Education (1989) *PE for Children with Special Educational Needs in Mainstream Education*, Leeds: White Line Press.

# Chapter 3

# The Range of Alternatives for Provision

Ideally we are aiming for the physically disabled child to be fully integrated at all times. In practice this might not be feasible nor advisable and this fact is fully acknowledged in the NC. Finding the right balance is essential for everyone concerned.

Generally it is found that virtually all children in Key Stages 1 and 2 can be happily and successfully integrated into class lessons, albeit by considering variations in task, response, or equipment, or by using an extra helper. Full involvement of the 'special' child is sometimes achieved by re-thinking some of the teaching methods and organizational details for the whole group. In these cases not only that individual, but also a significant percentage of the class who are underachievers should also benefit, e.g. small-sided games invariably demand more involvement and interaction, of more youngsters, and are therefore more appropriate than the adult 11-a-side game of football or 7-a-side netball game. However, any of the range of alternatives might need to be used at some time, so should be borne in mind.

In Key Stages 3 and 4, it can sometimes be much harder and less relevant for the child to follow the traditional curriculum, particularly where major team games are involved. Individual activities such as gym, dance, aerobics, swimming, weight-training, table-tennis and trampolining are often more worthwhile and easier to integrate into. The range of possible alternatives is charted in Figure 2. Of course there should be infinite flexibility, so that the disabled youngster is meaningfully integrated wherever possible, e.g. a wheel-chair bound lad of 12 may attend a local leisure centre for fitness training during his group's rugby session, swim with them in their school's or the local pool, and work alongside his peers in athletics, sometimes using elements of his own modified programme of activities. Even if separate or substituted activities are sometimes thought to be preferable, this might not be true throughout the week, or the school year, as the example illustrates.

B

**Figure 2** Alternative forms of provision

| Type | Notes |
| --- | --- |
| 1. Integrated | No special considerations are needed apart from constant re-appraisal by the teacher that the child really is integrated, beyond the level of just being present in the group, and that he or she is actively gaining from the session. |
| 2. Integrated plus helper | The helper needs to be aware of all relevant information about the child and to be clear exactly what is expected of him or her. Be watchful that the well-meaning helper, by being constantly in attendance, is not actually stifling independence and decision-making. A fine balance is needed. Helpers might be volunteer parents or dinner ladies, sixth-formers, students or ancillaries. Check your Authority's position regarding insurance here. |
| 3. Integrated but modified | The child works alongside his or her peers, often with a helper, but modifications are made to either:<br>a. the equipment used,<br>b. the rules, or<br>c. the response expected,<br>   e.g. a larger, softer ball may be preferable to a hockey ball; a football might be 'dribbled' by using the small front wheels of a wheelchair. |
| 4. Parallel | Although working in the same environment, different tasks might be set or activities presented, e.g. wheelchair obstacle courses can be negotiated alongside games skills training and involve work on similar aspects of skill acquisition. |
| 5. Separate | Alternative, segregated activities can be provided for individuals or small groups either instead of, or in addition to, class sessions. If the latter, they can sometimes be used to practise skills needed in the class lesson, as well as providing opportunity to try a number of the different options outlined. These are discussed in detail in Chapter 4. |
| 6. Use of alternative venues | Local leisure centres or special schools, for example, may have facilities which would extend the range of activities normally available within the child's own school. A good example here is the hydrotherapy or swimming pool. |
| 7. Contract system | It may be possible to negotiate a contract between the child and his or her teachers so that regular attendance at an activity outside school, e.g. evening swimming club, is accepted as curriculum work 'in exchange' for attendance at rugby, netball or whatever is the inappropriate session. |

In general terms, the more severe the disability the greater the need for an individualized programme and for individual instruction, but again there are no set rules and flexibility is essential. The overriding principle for all should be that participation is always in the least restrictive, least segregated environment as is practicable at that time.

Fostering a positive partnership with parents could prove extremely beneficial here, since not only could they be of great practical help and support, but parental attitudes have the potential for greatly affecting the successful outcome of any planned PE activities.

# Chapter 4

# Dimensions of the Subject

However PE is organized in your school, whatever the age of children taught and regardless of any of the alternative forms of provision which may be included, it is important that every individual disabled child experiences as wide a range of activities as is feasible and practical. It is also important that his or her own personal programme is well balanced and covers the areas specified in the NC wherever possible, as well as being challenging and rewarding. This balance needs to be both in terms of the type of activity and the physical demands made of the child, and in the involvement of others together with the type of environment in which the activity takes place, for example, balancing the demands for strength with precision; for speed with endurance; for solitary with group activities; for competitive elements with cooperative skills. Often this will be achieved by using a combination of traditional and more specialist activities, which are now outlined.

These less well known, specialist areas may be used as the 'substitute activities', as suggested by the Working Party, if aspects of the NC are unsuitable. Also, many serve to develop skills which then contribute to, or enhance performance in, the traditional or NC subject areas, or use skills which are components of these activities and so should be recognized as acceptable forms of activity within the programme of study. Others, such as wheelchair dancing, are alternative forms of the specified statutory activity so also merit inclusion.

## Traditional activities

### Gymnastics and dance

It is probably in these areas, more than any other, that full integration and worthwhile participation are possible, despite significant individual differences and very varied mobility and ability levels. Since these forms of movement education are primarily about extending the movement potential of the individual, each child should be able to perform at his or her own level within the class environment and gain pleasure from his or her achievements.

These areas are especially beneficial for physically disabled youngsters to experience since so many important skills in which they are often deficient can be mastered or developed, such as body awareness, spatial awareness, balance, coordination, rhythm and timing. Many of the important, specific aims of PE, as already outlined, can be tackled through the movement education programmes of study, which are particularly relevant and worthwhile for youngsters in Key Stages 1 and 2. Dance, which can be participated in using a variety of mobility aids including the wheelchair, is especially beneficial for a number of children with special educational needs, since it provides a nonverbal form of communication and opportunity for creativity and expression of moods and feelings.

## Games

In general, games pose more problems for children with physical disabilities than other areas, but often they can be enjoyed and participated in with enthusiasm if appropriate modifications and adaptations can allow for fair and true participation. However, the substitute activities might well be more appropriate for children whose mobility is severely impaired or who have very limited coordination.

By the very nature of the activity, games situations are complex since rules, tactics and equipment have all to be taken into account, together with an ever-changing environment. Understanding of the activity and the necessary level of anticipation and skill are needed, as well as basic body management. Sometimes taking part in a full game may not be feasible, but much can be gained from working in small games and on simplified activities, whilst developing the key skills from the major game. Cooperation and competition, tactics and skill can all be fostered in a 2-a-side game as well as in an 11-a-side match! Using a whole range of small apparatus and different types of games settings are valuable too, to put games skill learning into meaningful contexts.

Games can be classified into one of three types:

- running or invasion games such as rugby, basketball, netball and football are probably the hardest for the disabled child to play alongside his or her peers, although there is much to be gained from mastering the different skills involved, and using them in game-like situations;
- over-the-net games like badminton and volleyball are often more appropriate, especially if some minor modifications to rules or equipment are made;
- striking and fielding games such as rounders and cricket can often be enjoyed, using the above modifications, and by paying careful attention to which positions are played.

## Athletics

Since the vast majority of athletics events are of an individual nature, mixed participation is quite possible. The basic elements of running, jumping and throwing are enjoyed by most youngsters in Key Stages 1 and 2, and tasks can be loosely interpreted to make them accessible for all children. For example, a 'jump' could be the distance covered by placing crutches down once and swinging the legs through to land safely, or that covered by a wheelchair after one push; throws can be made from a standing, sitting or kneeling position, or even by the feet. These elements of basic skills can be refined into formal events at a later stage, which are still equally accessible to all. Award schemes are now available which aim to introduce and promote integrated athletics by the provision of some recognized modifications and specially formulated scoring tables (see Appendix A).

With the recent growth and recognition of athletics for the disabled, any interested youngster should be able to find coaching available locally and a range of local, regional and national competitions, most commonly organized by the British Sports Association for the Disabled, but also by specific disability groups such as Cerebral Palsy Sport (see Appendix C). The serious wheelchair-bound athlete will ultimately need his or her own sports wheelchair if he or she is to enter competition, and help with training, as would any athlete.

## Water activities/swimming

Water is probably the most satisfying, rewarding environment in which a physically disabled child can work and for some it will be the only place where total independence of movement is achieved. Activity in water can allow performance of movements which would otherwise be impossible and can, therefore, raise confidence and motivate further progress and allow for much learning about the body's capabilities. Swimming is also one of the most beneficial forms of exercise for anyone and hydrotherapy can be valuable to many. Therefore, every effort should be made to give disabled youngsters regular access to a swimming pool, whether they attend with their class group, or as an alternative arrangement. Virtually all children can participate in some form of water activity and gain intense physical and psychological benefits; but warmer-than-usual water is required for many, especially those who are immobile – around 94°F being recommended.

## Recreational and leisure pursuits

Although often less physically demanding, recreational or leisure activities are thoroughly worthwhile for older pupils and can be equally as challenging as other activities. Many are participated in individually and so are most appropriate for disabled teenagers. Also, developing an interest in recreational activities whilst at school may provide a pursuit for leisure time after school, a means of socializing and an encouragement to take up some form of physical activity voluntarily, so increasing the chances of maintaining physical well-being. Snooker, darts, bowls, archery, table-tennis and horse-riding are all activities which could profitably be included in a school's recreational activities or PE programme and so also provide education for leisure: the majority of activities are accessible to most disabled youngsters or adults, often without any special considerations being needed.

## Outdoor education

Learning through the outdoors (outdoor education) can involve young people in many outdoor pursuits which are within the capabilities of children with a

1 Outdoor education.

Outdoor education need not only take place over remote and rugged terrains – the local environment can hold interesting challenges.

disability, and prove to be intensely challenging and rewarding. However, not all activities are appropriate for all youngsters and extremely high levels of planning, organization and supervision will be required. It must be remembered that many physically disabled children feel the cold more intensely and tire more quickly than their peers and should never be put in situations of risk because of this. Nevertheless, a wide range of outdoor pursuits could be made available to the atypical child, should he or she wish it, and here again the school may well foster an interest which is pursued through adult life.

## Specialist areas

### Wheelchair events

There are a number of activities designed especially for the child who is wheel-chair-bound:

- racing
- slalom
- proficiency (see Appendix A)
- obstacle courses
- dancing
- games, e.g. basketball

The first four of these can make use of any available space, such as corridors or paved spaces, not necessarily PE areas where others are working, and facilities such as doors, ramps and chairs, as well as small games equipment. Such events are invariably most enjoyable for the child, whilst also developing confidence and manoeuvrability in the chair, physical prowess, independence skills and games playing ability. Challenges for the child to compete against him or her self, or against others with similar abilities, can easily be formulated, incorporating specific skills which need to be mastered, if appropriate; for example, straight reversing; opening doors and carrying objects through; turning on the spot; ducking under barriers. Manual or electric wheelchairs can be used for these activities. Ambulant children may choose to use a wheelchair to try participating in these events, which is to be encouraged since invariably the constant wheelchair user will be *more* skilful – probably for the only time in his or her life. It may also be possible for a group of disabled youngsters to gather together and play their own form of a highly specialized game such as wheelchair basketball, an opportunity which should not be denied them if interest and potential are shown. The activity should be recognized as providing a valid games element of the PE programme.

### Circuit training

Wheelchair-bound children can participate either in or out of their chairs, as appropriate, and since again the individual is only competing against him or her

2 Wheelchair slalom.

Wheelchair slalom and obstacle courses can be both demanding and great fun, whilst providing vital practice in wheelchair proficiency skills.

self, groups of children of very mixed ability can all profitably work together. Timing how long it takes to complete a set number of repetitions, or performing as many as possible within a set time are the two alternative methods of running a circuit. Specific skills can be developed, certain muscle groups strengthened or basic fitness and stamina trained, depending on the needs of the group and of individuals within it. Children should be encouraged to develop their own timing and scoring systems and recording sheets and should be responsible for their own scoring wherever possible: there is great potential here for a data-collection exercise and analysis of results.

Children can easily work in pairs if there are insufficient 'stations' for each to work alone. Rest periods may need to be built in for some individuals, or the timing reduced on certain activities so that children at risk do not become overtaxed. Although careful planning and good organization are prerequisites here, this is recommended as an excellent activity for involving quite large groups of children with very mixed ability and fitness levels and for producing excellent work rates. Children love to repeat the circuit at a later date and aim to improve their scores: progress can easily be charted.

### Weight training

Weight lifting should never be attempted by physically disabled school children, but weight training, when carefully supervised by an adult knowledgeable in both the activity and his or her subjects, can be a very profitable experience. Specific muscle groups used for everyday skills can be strengthened, so improving the individual's capacity for independence; for instance, wheelchair users need strong arm muscles for pushing their chair and for transferring into and out of it. Specialist equipment is not essential: beanbags, cans of food and medicine balls are all just as useful.

### New Games

The whole concept of 'New Games' is one of cooperation not competition, with totally unified participation from all members of the group being necessary for the goal or activity to be achieved. Probably the best known example of cooperative sport is parachute games which are rapidly increasing in popularity, but a whole host of activities are available (see Appendix B) or are

3 Parachute play.

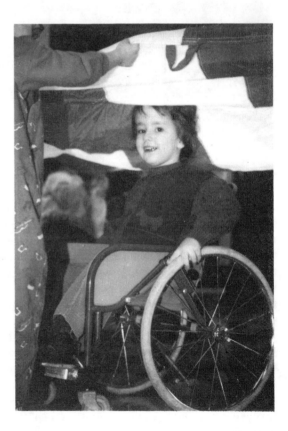

Parachute games being enjoyed in an integrated nursery.

easily created by imaginative adults or children alike. Because all members of the group need to be involved for it to be successful, great sensitivity develops between group members; New Games are ideal for the 'special' child to work in a fully integrated setting and are invariably enjoyed by both able-bodied and disabled alike of all ages. They can be made as simple or complex as required and as physically challenging as is appropriate for the various members of the group.

## Relationship play

Relationship play is a form of developmental movement made famous by Veronica Sherborne – it is sometimes called Sherborne Movement. This develops the child's ability to relate to him or her self and to others by enabling him or her to become very aware of the capabilities of his or her own body. It is as suitable for mainstream children as it is for those 'special' children who have learning difficulties, physical difficulties or behavioural abnormalities and has often been successfully used to promote integrated activities. Sherborne's approach to movement development depends on working in a one-to-one relationship, with one of the pair being the more mature, or more able, but both invariably gaining from the experiences. An infinite variety of pairings are possible, but suggestions include

| | |
|---|---|
| senior pupils | + disabled youngsters |
| voluntary helpers | + mixed ability class group |
| teachers | + disabled individuals |

Relationships are developed progressively through caring or 'with' activities, shared experiences and finally, when trust in each other has been fully established, 'against' activities testing strength and stability. Through relationship play, body awareness, communication, physical skills, self-concept and emotional security can all be developed, therefore also being beneficial to, and complementary to, other areas of the PE curriculum.

## Sports appreciation

There will be occasions when active involvement is impossible for some children. Nevertheless, an active role can be played in the session, if becoming a 'knowledgeable spectator' is recognized as a worthwhile pursuit and is encouraged. Developing an awareness of quality in performance, of tactics, rules and time-keeping may allow the child to play the role of coach, judge, referee or scorer and so to be fully involved at his or her own level with his or her peers and to show both knowledge and understanding of the activity. Using radio and TV programmes, video recordings of national events and trips to sporting occasions, as well as in-school lessons, all help to develop sports appreciation and the 'informed spectator' concept, so that contributions to the school PE programme can be made and sports can also be enjoyed as a leisure activity, out of school.

# Chapter 5

# Disabling Conditions

Medical aspects of the most frequently encountered conditions are now discussed so that the implications for PE can be identified, recognized and appreciated. As well as the noted physical, sensory or medical disability, the teacher needs to be fully alert to a range of 'hidden' or associated difficulties which can have just as significant effects on the learning process. These may include:

- Lack of early movement experience, poor body awareness and under-standing of action words.
- Difficulties with hand–eye coordination.
- Problems with attending and concentrating.
- Hyperactivity and distractability.
- Spatial and perceptual difficulties.
- Problems with rhythm, sequencing and organization.

## Arthritis (Still's disease)

Primarily affecting the joints but sometimes involving other systems of the body too, such as vision, rheumatoid arthritis is a common and chronic inflammatory condition of unknown origin; in children it is sometimes known as Still's disease. Affected joints, most commonly the hands and feet, but some-sometimes knees and elbows too, become swollen and tender, with thickening of surrounding tissues and restrictions to mobility causing pain. During remissions the symptoms subside, but the disease is a progressive one. Rest is needed in acute cases, otherwise joints could become further damaged and more pain be caused, but normally joints need to be put through their full range of movement to prevent them becoming fixed.

## Implications for PE

Still's disease can be extremely painful and sufferers should not be allowed nor encouraged to try any movements which aggravate the pain.

Any activity which could cause twisting or jarring to the knees and ankles, such as jumping, should be avoided even when the disease is in remission.

Control of equipment might be impeded if hand and finger joints are affected and grasp is limited.

Swimming is the best form of exercise since no weight-bearing is involved and warm water is relaxing to painful joints.

## Asthma

Asthma is one of the most chronic diseases of childhood. It can be described as laboured, wheezing breathing caused by interference of the normal flow of air into and out of the lungs due to the decreased diameter of the airways. Shortness of breath and coughing are often present, as muscles of the airways contract causing spasm and tissues become swollen and irritated. Attacks can vary from the very mild to the most severe, in which case prompt medical attention is required. Treatment is usually by drugs, often in the form of an inhaler, which work by dilating the airways and can be either preventative or used as a relief from attacks.

Some asthma attacks are triggered by specific features such as certain foods, drugs, dust or pollen, by a virus, extreme temperature changes or excessive exercise; sometimes there appears to be no definite cause. Attacks can be very distressing to the child and those around him or her, so calm reassurance and management are needed by the supervising adults.

## Implications for PE

- Asthma should not be used as an excuse to avoid PE but teachers should appreciate a child's anxiety about taking part. Discussions with the child and his or her parents should prove helpful.
- Prolonged activity is worse for asthmatic children than short bursts; so too are cold, dry conditions worse than warm, damp ones. Alternative arrangements to outside lessons may need to be made on certain days.
- Any trigger features must of course be known and avoided: work on grass, especially just after it has been cut, may be unwise.
- Many children manage the likelihood of an asthma attack by using their inhalers 15 minutes before beginning to exercise; for all children, a thorough warm-up to any activity is vital.
- Teachers should be aware that there appears to be a direct relationship between the amount of effort being expended and the likelihood of breathing problems resulting. However, asthmatic children tend to have poor general health, posture and fitness and therefore do need to take part in regular exercise.

- Swimming is excellent for these children provided the water is neither too warm nor too cold and that short bursts of work rather than prolonged activity are encouraged.

## Brittle bones (Osteogenesis imperfecta)

This is an inherited condition, varying very much in its severity, in which there is an inborn abnormality in the structure of the protein component of bone. Ligaments may also be lax and hearing problems can be present too. Fracture can occur with frightening simplicity, for example when turning over in bed, and although they usually heal normally, frequent fractures can result in deformities. The most severe cases cause a shortening in stature and affected children are permanently wheelchair-bound.

### Implications for PE

- The child who has brittle bones should not be allowed to participate in any form of contact sports.
- Swimming is an ideal form of exercise, but care must be taken when entering and leaving the water and supervision is necessary.
- The child could be vulnerable in crowded changing rooms, or when moving around as part of a crowd: alternative arrangements might have to be made.
- It would be wise to plan the PE programme in consultation with the physiotherapist. The role of 'knowledgeable spectator' will probably prove useful here, but not to the exclusion of the child's own activity, in some form and as varied as possible.

## Cerebral palsy

Cerebral palsy (CP) is the name used for a group of non-progressive disorders of posture and movement which are caused by damage or injury to the developing brain. The vast majority of cases, whose incidence is approximately 2 children per 1,000, relate to pregnancy and birth trauma, with asphyxia, neonatal jaundice and prematurity being the most common. Postnatal causes include trauma, infection and high fever.

There are three main types of CP, depending on the area of the brain damaged, and children usually have one condition dominant but may well show a mixture to some degree. No two children are affected in the same way, especially since each type can range from a minor to a very severe manifestation. Spasticity, the most common type, results from damage to the motor cortex and leads to increased muscle tone and stiff but weak muscles. Abnormal postures occur, which cause deformity unless constantly corrected. Athetoid children show involuntary 'writhing' movements which become even more marked when voluntary activity is attempted and therefore distort purposeful activity; hearing loss may be present too. Athetosis results from damage to the

**Figure 3**  Terminology according to limb involvement

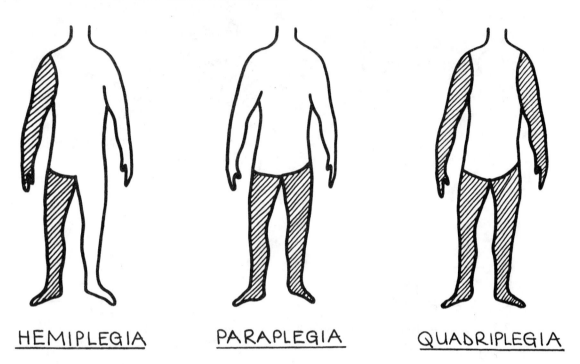

HEMIPLEGIA          PARAPLEGIA          QUADRIPLEGIA

basal ganglia. Because the cerebellum is affected in ataxic children they show disturbances in balance and clumsy or uncoordinated voluntary movements. As any or all of the limbs may be involved, a further classification 'by distribution' is made (see Figure 3), but it is very important to remember that head and body movements are also affected.

Associated with the motor disorders there may well be one or more of the following disabilities: hearing or visual impairment; speech impediments; perceptual or concentration difficulties; and epilepsy. Secondary handicaps can also develop because of any restrictions a child with CP may meet in normal exploratory and learning experiences and opportunities for socialization.

## Implications for PE

- There is a great tendency for a child with CP to deteriorate in physical efficiency, unless he or she takes part in some form of systematic physical activity.
- Because of the wide ranging nature of the condition, teachers need to use both 'performer analysis' and 'task analysis' to make sure that the activity is carefully matched to the child's movement ability.
- Functional ability is much more important than style and sometimes quite prolonged sessions of experimentation, with teachers and child working together, may be necessary to finally decide upon the most appropriate positioning and approach to a task.

**Figure 4**  Functional positioning for spastic children

## STANDING

i) Feet flat
ii) Hips and knees straight
iii) Elbows straight; hands down
iv) Head in midline
v) Weight evenly distributed over both feet.

## SITTING

i) Feet flat on floor or support
ii) Bent hips and knees
iii) Bottom well back in chair
iv) Head in midline

## FLOOR SITTING

i) Discourage 'W' leg position
ii) Encourage side - sitting or long - sitting positions, with weight taken through straight arms, with hands flat on floor.

- Spastic children need careful positioning, with spasm minimized, to enable them to perform to best advantage (see Figure 4). Spasm can be increased by fear, excitement or tiredness and loud noises can lead to a sudden 'startle reflex', in which grasp and postural control may be lost.
- Fast movements are on the whole inappropriate because where the child has spasticity they encourage use of the worst motor patterns and athetoid and ataxic children seldom have the motor control to achieve them; effort makes control harder, too.
- Periods of relaxation at the start of lessons will probably produce better performances in spastic children.
- Spatial, perceptual and organizational problems are common and could severely affect a child's performance in PE, but could also be improved by specific training within PE sessions.
- Dressing and undressing can often cause difficulties, which can partly be alleviated by allowing plenty of time, providing a calm, quiet environment and helping with sorting and organization.
- Grasping and releasing objects tend to be slower and more of a challenge than normal and moving objects can therefore be very difficult to deal with.
- Day-to-day performance may fluctuate if the child is very stressed, tired, or 'under the weather'. Even on a good day, a tremendous amount of effort often has to be expended for the child to be able to perform even basic skills to his or her satisfaction, and teachers need to remember this.
- Swimming in warm water is excellent for children with CP since it is a real aid for relaxing tight muscles. However, cold water can increase spasm, so it must be avoided. Breath control is very difficult since there is a natural tendency to inhale, rather than exhale, particularly if a child is startled; exercises to practise controlled breathing out, such as blowing balloons along, could be helpful.
- The child's physiotherapist or occupational therapist should be able to provide much helpful advice about positioning, recommended and contra-indicated activities and general management. Therapy aims should be incorporated into the PE programme so that both are complementary – therapy is much more fun when included unobtrusively into a group game than when it has to be tackled as a sterile exercise!

## Clumsiness

Clumsiness is not a single syndrome but a description of a range of diverse symptoms, characterized by disorganization of movement, which seem to arise from problems with perceiving sensory input and organizing motor responses. More prevalent in boys than girls, clumsiness affects between 5 and 10 per cent of the school population. Every class is therefore likely to include a clumsy child. Clumsy children are a heterogenous group, (there being no typical clumsy child) with no overt signs of disability but nevertheless needing as much help and understanding since subtle disruptions to learning result and because so much of everyday life depends on motor skill. Gross or fine motor skills can be affected and one or more of the following: rhythm, balance, spatial aware-nes; perceptual integrity; directionality, organizational and sequencing ability.

Children who are clumsy are also often unfit and hypotonic, with hypermobile joints, so acquiring motor skills can be extremely difficult for them.

Without intervention clumsy children can be scolded by teachers, scorned by peers and be a disappointment to parents, so that secondary emotional or social problems develop, or avoidance tactics such as playing the class fool are brought into play. Clumsy children are therefore very deserving of our help and attention. Motor impairment is out of all proportion to general ability, so there is often a definite awareness of failure and self-image/self-esteem invariably suffer; associated behaviour problems such as hyperactivity, short attention span and emotional lability are common, too. It is important to intervene early and treat the disability, but to identify also abilities which can be developed to ensure success and so give the self-confidence for proficient learning.

### Implications for PE

- PE is often the most dreaded lesson, but can also be the session where the clumsy child receives most help, if the teacher is fully aware and understanding of what life can be like for a clumsy child.
- A sympathetic approach and a carefully structured programme in which skills are taught through finely graded steps can do much to improve performance and so raise self-esteem.
- Individual activities, such as gym and dance, in which responses can be made at a person's own level, are easiest for the clumsy child to participate in; sensitive handling by the teacher, or competitive situations, will be needed to avoid the feeling of failure being reinforced. All practice of balance, rhythm and coordination skills should prove beneficial, but handling moving objects will be difficult.
- Whilst aiming to improve basic skills by breaking them down into the simplest of stages, teachers should also help the child find ways of circumventing major problem areas.
- It is important to find areas where the child can find enjoyment and be successful which will help him or her improve in self-confidence and self-esteem and also develop basic fitness levels.

### Cystic fibrosis

Cystic fibrosis (CF) is a genetic disorder in which the mucous glands secrete abnormally thick mucus: the lungs and pancreas are primarily affected. This thick mucus which forms in the lungs is not naturally and easily moved up the bronchial tubes, so that it can build up causing infection or obstruction. Also, abnormal mucus in the pancreas prevents enzymes flowing freely from the pancreas into the small intestine and therefore impedes digestion of fats and protein. CF cannot yet be cured; careful daily management of the condition is required, including physiotherapy, postural drainage and drug therapy, to keep the bronchial tubes clear, prevent infection and aid digestion. A persistent cough is usually present.

## Implications for PE

- Exercise is good for the child with CF, to build up heart and lung capacity. PE should be encouraged but over-exertion avoided.
- Frequent absences due to chest infections may result in key areas of work or skills tuition being missed and teachers need to be sensitive to this.
- Persistent coughing and the clearing of mucus are facts of life for these children, therefore the opportunity to dispose of soiled tissues should be made available as unobtrusively as possible.
- Swimming in warm water is recommended since regular, rhythmic breathing is developed.

## Diabetes

With diabetes, the body does not manufacture sufficient of the hormone insulin to allow muscles to absorb glucose and so produce energy. Because glucose is not absorbed, levels rise causing thirst, frequent urination, weight loss and lethargy. Approximately 1 in 900 children under the age of 16 suffer from diabetes; its onset can be rapid and severe, with all of the above symptoms. Diabetes is treated by injection of insulin and dietary control to achieve a balance between insulin availability in the body and glucose uptake. Low glucose levels (hypoglycaemia) can result if the child does not eat sufficiently, is late for meals or is very energetic. This causes lack of concentration, sweating, pallor and shakiness, together with vomiting. The remedy is to give sugar in the form of sweets and biscuits, but this should never be attempted if the child is already comatose – immediate medical attention should then be sought. It is wise to keep a supply of sugary snacks available in school at all times.

## Implications for PE

- A diabetic child should normally be able to take part in PE alongside his or her peers, but medical advice should be obtained initially.
- A snack may be needed before starting any activity or midway through it. Although we should be encouraging the child to manage his or her condition independently, it is wise for the PE teacher to keep food stocks with them, particularly when supervising more strenuous events such as cross-country.
- Because it is so important that the child eats regularly and does not miss meals, particular care must be taken over the planning and organization of any school trips, outings or outdoor pursuits events.

## Epilepsy

'Electrical storms' or epileptic fits, caused by brief disruptions in the normal electrochemical activity in the brain, can affect people of all ages and intelligence, race and state of health. Fits take a variety of forms, the two most common being 'grand mal' and 'petit mal' seizures. Epilepsy is invariably controlled by drugs, usually without any side effects, but occasionally there may be some dulling of the faculties. Sometimes a child has a few moments warning of an impending fit, such as heightened perception or a strange feeling but this is not always the case.

Petit mal attacks are manifest as minor absences, which although only lasting a few seconds can nevertheless be distressing to the child and a handicap to learning, since vital instructions and information are missed. Minor eye movements can indicate the child is having a petit mal, but may go unnoticed. Grand mal attacks may last several minutes but should be left to run their course; hospital intervention is necessary if fits last more than 10–15 minutes, so the onset time of a fit should be noted, if possible. In a grand mal attack the child could lose consciousness and fall to the ground with stiffness in his or her arms and legs. This phase is followed by one of jerky spasms before the body finally relaxes. Bladder and bowel control may be lost and the child may well be drowsy or confused for some hours afterwards. To help manage a fit, only passive first aid is required, i.e., calmly reassure the child and those around him or her and remove any dangerous objects from the vicinity; loosen any clothing and place the child in a semi-prone position with his or her head to one side; do not attempt to put anything in his or her mouth.

**Implications for PE**

- All PE teachers should know of any epileptics in their classes and how to cope with a fit should one occur.
- Fits occur less often when the child is active and occupied but can be initiated by excitement or stress, as in competitions, or by inactivity. Flickering lights and reflections on water may also be trigger features.
- Work on high gym apparatus should be avoided, also cycling on roads, because of the hazard of falling under a car.
- In the swimming pool an epileptic child should have a one-to-one relationship with a responsible adult. If he or she is then included in the group activity it is helpful if some means of easy identification is used, for example, wearing a yellow swimming hat.
- It is important that drugs are taken at regular intervals, so any child being taken out of school for outings or events must take his or her medication with him or her.

## Friedrich's ataxia

Causing a progressive deterioration of coordination and muscle control, Friedrich's ataxia (FA) is a relatively rare, inherited disease of the central nervous system, due to a genetic disorder. FA usually begins to become apparent in the early teenage years, when a general clumsiness and poor balance may be noticed. As the leg muscles first become affected, a wide, 'drunken' gait is adopted; later loss of control in arm and hand muscles causes difficulty in precise, fine movements and may be accompanied by a tremor. Vision, speech and hearing can ultimately be affected too. Children with FA may also have the associated problems of poor circulation, occasional heart palpitations and diabetes with which to contend.

## Implications for PE

- The junior school years are usually completed without the need to use any mobility aids. Later the gradual introduction to use of a wheelchair will have to be sensitively managed – teenagers could well be intensely embarrassed, frustrated and upset by their increasing dependence on others. Much can be done through PE to develop wheelchair skills.
- Regular exercise is needed to maintain mobility and levels of functioning. The child's physiotherapist should be able to make suggestions and advise regarding PE. Swimming is thoroughly recommended.
- As with any deteriorating condition, teachers working with a child with FA should constantly review the situation and liaise with others involved with its management, so that the child is always suitably challenged, not overtaxed, and gains appropriate movement experience from the PE programme.

## Hearing impairment

The effect on a child of any form of hearing impairment (HI) depends very much on the degree and type of hearing loss and time of its onset. There are two main forms of HI – conductive deafness, resulting from infection, obstruction or malformation of the outer or middle ear; and sensori-neural deafness, in which there is damage to the inner ear or auditory nerve itself. In the former case, deafness may be persistent or intermittent and most frequently caused by inner-ear infections; in the latter situation, deafness may be permanent and severe but sometimes alleviated to some extent by various forms of hearing aids. However, it must be remembered that aids amplify all sound and therefore do not necessarily make speech clearer. Depending on the degree and time of onset of the HI, speech and language development, and therefore concept formation too, may be severely impeded. Some children use lip-reading to compensate for hearing loss, others are taught a signing system for communication. The majority will be supported to some extent by a peripatetic teacher of the HI, who should also be available to support and advise staff.

## Implications for PE

- PE is very beneficial since it provides an outlet for non-verbal expression and aids language and concept development.
- Communication difficulties are the biggest problem for you and the child with HI. Be prepared for frustration, misunderstanding and confusion and make sure that the child is never at risk.

- If the child uses lip-reading, stand still facing him or her, with the light on your face, not behind you. Use normal rhythm and intonation when talking to him or her or to the group. When a signing system is practised, teachers should make the effort to at least learn key words, to use along-side speech.
- Alert the child to visual cues which you and he or she can develop as a communication system, in conjunction with language. Use demon-strations to illustrate what is expected and reduce unnecessary language. Remember that warning signs will not be heard.
- Sometimes a specialist may advise against swimming, if there has been middle ear infection, or actual damage such as a perforated ear drum. Contact in the swimming pool, where the child cannot use his or her aids and there is a lot of extraneous noise, is particularly difficult – it could be made through a considerate and watchful friend.
- Hearing aids can be worn for PE as long as they are fitted securely.

## Heart conditions

The most common form of heart conditions are congenital, with 'hole-in-the-heart' defects, varying very much in severity, being the most frequently encountered. Sometimes heart problems are associated with other conditions such as Down's syndrome. Because of the wide range of defects possible, their differing effects in individual children and of the possible life-threatening nature of severe conditions, no generalizations regarding PE should be made – each child must be treated as an individual.

### Implications for PE

- No PE should be undertaken without a letter from the child's doctor giving clear indication of what activity is permissible.
- The child's parents should be consulted from the outset and possible activity discussed with them.
- Do not rely on the child knowing his or her limitations and asking to stop when necessary; be alert for watchpoints too.
- Watch for shortness of breath, unusual fatigue, blueness around the lips and nail beds; stop the activity immediately.
- Teachers must know of the exercise tolerance level.
- Children with heart conditions sometimes feel the cold more than usual, so outdoor activities might not always be appropriate. Similarly, swimming in a hydrotherapy pool which is too warm can become over-taxing, so should not be pursued for too long.
- In general, short spells of activity which are interspersed with rest periods are recommended. The child should not be urged on to produce greater speed or effort, nor to work harder at endurance. The excitement caused by team games should be monitored, too.

## Muscular dystrophy

Characterized by a progressive weakness of all muscle groups, muscular dystrophy (MD) is an inherited disease which more frequently affects boys but can also be seen in girls. The most common type, called Duchenne muscular dystrophy, is carried through the female line, but only manifests in boys; approximately 1 in 3,000 male births show the disease. A peculiar, waddling gait, walking on the toes, clumsiness or poor posture with sway back and protruding abdomen may be the first indication that anything is wrong. Usually the child remains on his or her feet until some time towards the end of his or her primary school years, but even then, standing up from the floor or climbing stairs may be beyond his or her capabilities. A manual wheelchair will in time need to be replaced by an electric one which still allows the child to retain some independence.

As the muscle cells lose their power and degenerate and are replaced by fat and connective tissue, muscles may appear unusually large, especially those in the calf and thigh. Restricted activity may also contribute to obesity, but occasionally MD results in marked wasting. In the later stages of the disease, joint contractions are common because of uneven weakness in muscles and splints may be needed to help prevent and overcome deformity. Because the child has no tone in his or her muscles and weakness in his or her shoulder girdle, he or she will be very difficult to lift and should not be pulled up by the hands or from under the arms. His or her physiotherapist can advise on the best techniques to use, which may involve two people when the dystrophy is in an advanced stage.

### Implications for PE

- Although the child is weak and getting weaker, PE is undoubtedly beneficial, and is actively sought by the vast majority of those with MD. PE can actually help overcome, or correct, disuse atrophy caused by inactivity and lack of muscle use.
- The child with MD should be encouraged to use his or her full range of movements, for as long as possible, without tiring him or her unnecessarily; he or she will tire easily.
- Include him or her in all aspects of PE, gradually and sensitively introducing adaptations and alternatives where necessary, but also ensuring that participation in group activities is both possible and enjoyable.
- Be prepared for verbal outbursts and temper, as frustration builds up with a growing awareness of increasing limitations. If possible, provide some outlet for it, e.g. a punch bag.
- Coordination is unimpaired, so ball and racquet games, using suitably light equipment, are particularly appropriate. Snooker is invariably popular, and table-tennis might be enjoyed too. Hockey sticks can be fixed to the front of electric chairs!
- Swimming is probably the best form of exercise and sessions in warm water are excellent for relaxation too. It is the activity which can be

carried on the longest and the one which allows the greatest degree of independence, so it should always be included in the PE programme.

- When the disease is advanced, preparation for swimming involves considerable 'manhandling'. This should be done as sensitively as possible, so that the child is not deterred from the activity itself. Advice from his or her therapist will be invaluable here.
- Although independence in the water will be retained long after it is lost on land, watch that these children do not tip into face-down positions, from which they cannot right themselves, or that they cannot sit up from a floating position, particularly on their back. The youngsters themselves are usually quite clear whether they feel more comfortable on their fronts or backs and their views should be respected.

## Spina bifida and hydrocephalus

Literally 'split spine', spina bifida (SB) is a congenital abnormality caused by the bones of the spinal column not forming correctly and closing progressively over the spinal cord. Although various degrees of severity occur, it is usually the case that the spinal cord at the site of the defect is exposed and nerves at that level damaged. According to the level of the spinal malformation there will be varying degrees of lower limb and trunk muscle paralysis, loss of sensation, and often, too, inability to control the muscles of the bladder and bowel. Appliances may be used, or regular catheterization, to gain some degree of bladder control. Bones which are non-weight-bearing, and surrounded by atonic muscles, are particularly susceptible to fractures, and the lack of sensation means that the skin of the lower limbs is very vulnerable, especially when the child is wheelchair-bound and has poor circulation. Splints or calipers may be used for part of the day for walking practice, but many children with SB spend much of their time in their wheelchairs, so need frequent changes of position to prevent sores developing.

Spina bifida and hydrocephalus commonly occur together, but both can exist independently. Hydrocephalus (water on the brain) is caused by the build up of cerebro-spinal fluid in the ventricles of the brain, causing unnatural pressure. It is usually treated by the implantation of a valve or shunt into the brain, which allows excess fluid to drain away into the body cavity.

In children who have SB and hydrocephalus, spatial and perceptual problems are common and there may also be difficulties with manual dexterity and fine motor coordination; organizational skills and sequencing ability may be affected too. Eye defects and squints can be associated aspects of the disability. Many children exhibit 'cocktail party' chatter which is superficially mature, but may lack depth and mask real understanding. Obviously, SB and hydrocephalus are complex and multi-faceted conditions and the affected child has much with which to contend.

Headaches, drowsiness and vomiting may indicate that the valve or shunt is malfunctioning; immediate medical attention should be sought and parents informed. High temperatures could result from urinary infections or from an infected shunt, so these should be watched for also.

**Implications for PE**

- Exercise is vital for these children, to improve circulation and muscle tone and develop fitness and independence skills. Lack of exercise could easily exacerbate an already complex situation.
- Children with paralysis and lack of sensation are unaware of the position of their legs and can easily trap them in hazardous situations, such as under apparatus. They need to be taught to consider their legs at all times and teachers need to be especially vigilant. The best and safest way of moving along the floor is bottom-hotching backwards.
- Bare skin is inadvisable in floorwork sessions because of the risks of friction burns and grazes; similarly, socks should be worn when swimming and a watch kept for feet which may drag on the pool bottom. Pool entry must be carefully supervised to avoid damage to sensitive skin and fragile bones.
- Appliances must be emptied before the lesson and certain activities which could cause them to dislodge, such as pulling along on the stomach, might have to be avoided completely. Some exercises, such as strong work on abdominal muscles, often result in bowel movements. Many children, particularly when they are being trained to gain some bladder control, need to visit the loo very frequently and must be allowed to leave the lesson immediately they feel it is necessary.
- Extra care must be taken with children with shunts: the site of the shunt is vulnerable, and bangs to the head should be closely monitored. Forward rolls are not recommended by some paediatricians, as excessive pressure can be placed on the shunt.
- All activities which train wheelchair proficiency and independence are recommended, since it is through these that the SB child becomes confident in his or her own handling of the chair and is more able to cope with hazards he or she is likely to meet when out and about. However, work out of the wheelchair should be incorporated into the PE programme too.
- In the swimming pool, many children develop their own style which tends to use a rather wide stroke. Since this is necessary to maintain balance, it should be made as efficient as possible, but not corrected too drastically. Also, a better swimming position will usually be achieved with the head up, so balancing the tendency for the light, flaccidly paralysed lower limbs to float high in the water, causing tipping.

## Visual impairment

A number of different conditions cause visual defects, and there are many variations in the nature of the impairment; problems occur both in focusing and in the nature of the visual field itself. Specialists should be able to advise on the extent and specific nature of the sight loss, and therefore about the most appropriate teaching techniques to use, which could greatly improve a child's performance. Most children with visual impairment (VI) are supported in school by specialist peripatetic teachers who should also be available to relate to staff.

## Implications for PE

- There are seldom any restrictions placed on PE but anyone with a detached retina must avoid all jumping, diving and contact sports since these could cause further damage.
- If glasses are to be worn for PE they must have shatterproof lenses – obviously it is far better if the child can keep his or her glasses on, safely. Glasses can be worn for most water activities.
- Ideally the working area should be well-lit, but without glare or dazzle. If a lot of light enters from one place, it is helpful to the child with VI if he or she works with his or her back to it.
- Boundaries of working areas can be delineated by auditory or tactile clues to help the child orientate him or her self; it might be helpful to mark the edges of gym apparatus, ropes, etc. with yellow or luminous paint. The working area must of course be clear of all sharp edges or protrusions, especially those likely to cause tripping or damage to the head, which could be particularly hazardous to children with sight problems.
- Noisy, active games sessions can be very confusing and frightening and it is understandable that the child with VI may prefer to stay on the periphery.
- Let the individual children tell you which colour equipment is best for them – usually yellow is preferred but this is not always the case, and white or green might be chosen. Balls with bells or electronic bleepers inside are now available and of use with the severely impaired child; some will continue sounding even though the ball is stationary.
- Blind children require a stable environment so that they can learn their way around it: constant changes are too confusing, but with planned change, children learn to adapt to it.

    Remember that potentially dangerous situations might not be seen, so safe practice must always be insisted upon, together with extra vigilance from staff.
- Be alert to the problem of colour-blindness, which occurs most often in boys. Should it be present, take care not to cause embarrassment or confusion by inadvertent references to team colours or to coloured pieces of equipment.

# Chapter 6

# Questions to be Asked

Teachers need to gain considerable background information before they can be expected to include any physically disabled child in their teaching groups. Once they have this information, it should allow them to proceed with confidence and understanding, knowing that the safety and well-being of *all* their pupils are protected. I suggest that in the first instance an approach is made to the child's parents, and the proposed PE programme discussed with them, but a number of different professionals may also be able to provide valuable information and advice. Any or all of the following might need to be contacted:

school nurse
school medical officer
paediatrician
physio- or occupational therapist
support teacher
advisory teacher
educational psychologist
special school staff
specialist associations, e.g. Spastics Society
voluntary organizations, e.g. Riding for the Disabled

Answers are needed to the following questions.

## About the disability

### Is it inherited or acquired?

If the child has been disabled since birth, he or she has never known a period of normality and has no normal motor patterns on which to build. When a child becomes disabled during childhood, tremendous adjustments need to be made, but at least these are set against a background of normal experiences and development which can act as useful reference points.

### Is it caused by brain damage?

Some physical conditions are purely 'orthopaedic' and present as management problems, primarily. Where the disability is caused by damage to the brain, then a number of other problems to do with perception, attention control, organization and coordination may also be present. A brain-damaged child is often a multi-handicapped child, with subtle and hidden disabilities to contend with, as well as the obvious, physical disability.

### Is it likely to fluctuate or deteriorate?

Extremes of temperature, or marked temperature changes, can cause the child's condition to fluctuate. Similarly, excitement, anticipation, fear or loud noises may cause muscular control to worsen in some cases. Conditions which are intermittent, such as 'glue ear' must be watched out for, and those which are deteriorating need to be very sensitively managed, of course. Constant review of the situation is needed.

### Is the child on medication? Could performance be affected?

It is helpful to know which drugs are taken and when. If they need to be administered during school time, it must be decided who is to administer them. Some drugs can cause drowsiness and difficulties in concentrating.

### Is the child continent? How is incontinence managed?

Some children need to be allowed to use the toilet immediately they request it; for others, longer time than usual will have to be allowed for toiletting. A variety of methods can be used to cope with incontinence – the teacher should know which is being applied, since working in different positions and on certain movements may be contra-indicated, e.g. lying flat on the stomach and pulling yourself along is not recommended for anyone with a bag; concentrated work on abdominal muscles can result in bowel movements. The teacher in charge of each session needs to know whether any extra help is needed with toiletting and, if so, to arrange for it to be available.

## About teaching the subject

### Are all PE areas accessible?

If there are obvious problems, can these be overcome by adult help, the use of ramps, or by using alternative routes? Less obvious hazards to consider are such things as very long distances between locations, heavy double doors to open or door handles which cannot be reached by a child if in a wheelchair.

## Will extra time/help be needed?

Actually getting to the lesson from the other side of the school, changing and toiletting may all take more time for the disabled child than for the others, so appropriate plans need to be made. Leaving the previous lesson a few minutes early means that the child has quiet, empty corridors to negotiate – and a good chance of starting the PE session on time! He or she may then need to leave early, in order to prepare for the following activity. Help may well be needed with mobility, changing or toiletting so it should be made available sensitively and regularly.

## Are any activities particularly recommended?

Whatever work is done, it should at all times be complementary to any physio-therapy programme. Often specific therapy exercises can be easily and meaningfully incorporated into the PE activities and so practised in an enjoy-able and relevant situation. Certain activities are particularly recommended for children with certain disabilities, e.g. all arm-strengthening work is beneficial for children with paralysed legs; balancing skills of cerebral palsied or clumsy children can be enhanced through gym and dance, and receptive and expressive language developed through the same two activities, if children show delay here.

## Are any activities to be completely avoided?

PE must never aggravate the existing condition, nor put the child at risk. There-fore, epileptic children should be restricted from using high climbing apparatus; those with shunts (see under SB in Chapter 5) should not attempt forward rolls, and arthritic children must not jump if their knee joints are affected.

## Can normal PE kit be worn?

If the children have sensitive skins or lack sensation (for example, those with SB), then bare skin must be covered; jogging bottoms are often preferable to shorts, to protect the children and provide extra warmth. Where orthopaedic boots are normally worn, the physiotherapist may advise that they are kept on for PE sessions.

## Should calipers/boots/splints, etc. be taken off for PE?

Often the child knows for him or her self whether he or she can work better with or without the 'aid', and his or her views should be respected, once all the safety points relevant to the individual and his or her class-mates have been attended to. For example, if calipers and crutches are not to be used they must be left well clear of the working area so as not to be a hazard to others. Find out whether the child can manage to take off, and replace his or her aid independently; if not, learn how to assist.

**Can the child work out of his or her wheelchair? Can he or she manage to transfer him or her self?**

Once the guidelines are established, find out, also, how independent the child can be expected to be here. If assistance is likely to be needed, for both your sakes seek advice on how to lift safely.

## Recording relevant information

Having gained all this information, it is essential that not only is your knowledge shared with everyone currently teaching the disabled child, but also that it is passed on to new members of staff as he or she changes class or school. A clear, workable recording system is essential and a suggested outline for a personal profile is given in Figure 5. Remember to update this at regular intervals, or whenever the situation changes. In conjunction with this it will be necessary to consider whether the school's own subject and achievement records are appropriate to show the type of activities covered, and the progress made, by all participating children.

**Figure 5** Personal profile recording form

| Name: | D. of B: |
|---|---|
| Address :<br><br>Phone no: | G. P's Name and Address:<br><br>Phone no: |
| Disability: | Restrictions to movement: |
| Aids used: | Medication: |
| Hidden difficulties: | Fluctuations in condition:<br>WHEN<br><br>HOW |
| Limitations to learning: | Watchpoints / Special safety measures: |
| Other agencies involved:<br>NAME        CONTACT POINT | Other notes: |

# Chapter 7

# General Principles

Having found out all that it is possible to about the child's condition, his or her movement potential and movement needs, it is helpful to bear in mind a number of general principles. These should underpin all our work with children with special needs and so lead to their increased and more successful involvement.

## Focus on ability not disability

Establish the individual child's strengths and abilities and aim to develop these. Use areas where he or she is likely to be able to succeed – these may be in the less traditional activities – and make sure success is worthwhile, not trivial.

## Encourage independence

Check that the environment is organized to enhance this and that physically it does not impede independence. Also, provide opportunities for taking the initiative and for increasing independence in mobility and self-care areas. Specific skills training might be needed, for example, how to transfer from the wheelchair to the poolside; how to put on certain pieces of clothing.

## Encourage the child to be responsible for his or her own management and learning

The child needs to be able to sort out his or her own wheelchair, walking aids, kit or other equipment. If he or she needs help, they must be encouraged to ask for it appropriately, explaining what is needed, rather than waiting passively for assistance. He or she must be allowed to make decisions for him or herself, and if these turn out to be the wrong decisions, then enabled to see why this is so. Too many disabled youngsters have too much planned and done for them; PE is an excellent medium through which responsibility for learning can be developed and problem-solving opportunities met.

## Remember safety

Before any activity is started, be absolutely sure that all appropriate safety measures have been taken and that you are complying with your Authority's guidelines. Check that the environment is not in any way hazardous and that neither you, the disabled child, nor his or her classmates can in any way jeopardize the safety of others. For example, are you wearing any jewellery which could scratch the child as you support him or her? Are calipers and crutches left well out of the way of where others are working?

## Teach specific safety moves, routines or procedures

Through using this approach, wider opportunities and experiences will become available and independence should also be gained, for example, getting down from high apparatus or getting into the swimming pool, can be achieved by sitting with legs over the 'drop', turning onto the stomach and slowly lowering the legs, by bending at the hips, until the floor is felt or a safe position gained. Hands and arms can be used for support and anchorage (see Illustrations 4 and 5).

## Allow sufficient time

Remember that not only might more time be needed to prepare for the lesson, but also to understand and plan for the task and, most importantly, to complete it successfully.

## Be aware of specific 'watchpoints' for each child

Be thoroughly conversant with aspects of any task or features in the environment which should be avoided, for example, epileptic children should not use high climbing apparatus and may be affected by lights flickering on the swimming pool.

Also know of any signs or symptoms in the child which indicate that the activity is inappropriate, for example, children with a heart condition often turn blue around the lips when overtired.

4 Safety move off gym apparatus.

Reversing down safely off high apparatus where jumping is inappropriate; note the legs covered and the leg splint and orthopaedic boot kept on.

## Check understanding

It is important that time is taken to ensure that the child knows exactly what is expected of him or her – instructions may need to be simplified or demonstrations of the desired activity given.

5 Independent pool entry.

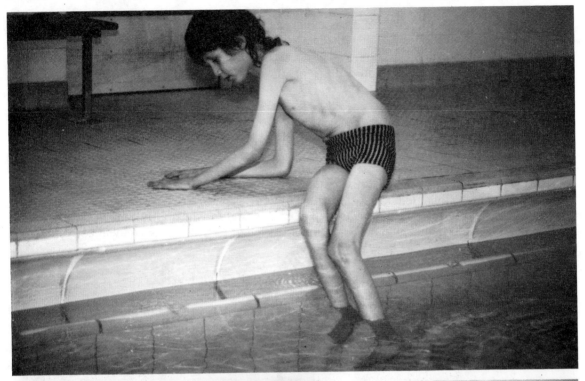

Getting into the swimming pool safely and independently, a method which is particularly good for protecting fragile legs.

### Appreciate the child's energy expenditure

Considerable effort is required by many children just to stay upright on their feet or to manoeuvre themselves around school, whether they use a wheelchair or not. The additional physical challenges within the PE lesson can be extremely demanding and tiring for the child, although theoretically within their capabilities.

### Use a variety of teaching styles

It may be necessary to extend your normal repertoire in order to be sure that the child appreciates what is wanted and is practising the desired skill correctly. Child and teacher demonstrations provide good visual images of what is wanted, and give examples of one way in which a task might be completed. Manual guidance may enable the child to 'feel' the movement correctly.

### Allow tasks to be met at the child's own level

If movement tasks are clearly and suitably set and not too specifically defined then all children in the group should be able to meet them appropriately, but at their own level. For example, 'practise forward rolls' could become 'practise rolling ensuring a smooth transfer of weight'.

### Recognize the value of close observation

Careful observation will help the teacher analyse the child's responses to the task and so make appropriate adjustments if necessary. Observing the *process* is more valuable than seeing the finished *product*, and provides more inform- ation to the teacher; for example, the way in which the child 'shapes up' to bat and actually hits the ball is more important than seeing the ball soaring in the air. Close observation of individuals should also alert the teacher to any situation in which the child might be 'at risk'.

### Make more specific use of language

Language can be used to check understanding of the task and then to plan, to rehearse and to reinforce the activity, if the child is allowed time to talk it through. Movement education is an excellent time to develop spatial and direct- ional concepts and ascertain understanding of them. For example, ask questions of the child such as 'Which direction are you going to move in?' and 'Which part of your body is highest?', as he or she works.

# Chapter 8
# Practical Tips

## General points

### Make use of an extra 'adult'

NNEBs, classroom ancillaries, support teachers, students, sixth-formers, parents, volunteers or peer tutors may all profitably be involved in facilitating integration into PE and access to appropriate challenges. Each must be clear what their duties are and exactly what is expected of them: an over-enthusiastic supporter may smother independence and be detrimental to the child, but a sympathetic, aware helper can be a tremendous ally to child and teacher alike.

### Modify the environment or work space

Larger, clearer areas may be needed in which to allow full wheelchair manoeuvrability, or smaller and restricted areas to prevent balls going out of reach.

### Modify the child's working position

A child with very poor balance may well prefer to use a wheelchair for active sessions, and be able to perform better from it. Similarly, a kneeling position may give him or her a more stable base than a standing one, and so allow fuller concentration on arm use and a more efficient action (see Illustration 6).

### Modify the task/response/apparatus/rules

These points are elaborated more fully in following sections.

6 Incorporating therapy into games playing.

A 'high-kneeling' position being used to improve participation in games play and to incorporate the therapy aims of developing balance and hip stability.

### Spend time in a wheelchair yourself

This is really the only way we can begin to appreciate what life is like for a wheelchair-bound child and whether what we are asking him or her to do is actually feasible and attainable.

### Encourage contact with parents

They may be able to give advice on handling or management, or warn of problem areas which the child might be reluctant to mention. Skills might be tackled at school and not at home, or vice versa, so a sharing, mutually supportive approach could be advantageous to all involved.

## Subject Specific – Games

### Avoid elimination games

Invariably the children who need most practice, for whatever reason, will be out first.

### Avoid children choosing their own teams

It is never nice to be the child who is left to last, whom the others clearly do not want to have on their team. This may well not be the child with an obvious disability, for which allowances are made, but the one with a hidden difficulty, such as clumsiness, which is less well understood by his or her classmates.

### Avoid pairing two special needs children together for ball skills practice

Each needs the practical support of a good 'feeder' who can reliably send the ball to the correct place, not always the moral support of another child also experiencing difficulties. Nor should the same peer-tutor always be used – they also need to develop their own skills at an appropriate level.

### Teach essential, specialist skills

Children who are wheelchair-bound need to be taught specific 'key' skills such as how to pick up a ball from the floor whilst their chair is still moving, i.e., by pushing the ball in against the rim of the wheel and allowing the wheel's rotation to bring the ball up to waist level; how to travel in their chair whilst carrying a stick or ball – imagination and adaptability are needed here; there are no hard and fast rules.

### Vary the equipment

Consider whether bats which are smaller, lighter, have larger handles or are shorter might be more appropriate. Beanbags are easier to release than balls; balloons or beachballs are so light they remain in the air longer and can be tracked more easily; foam balls of different density are also slower moving and

7 Selection of balls now available.

A selection of the wide variety of balls now available from many of the educational suppliers. The largest balls have great potential and are particularly useful pieces of equipment.

less painful to handle. Different coloured balls or other pieces of equipment may be preferable for some children.

## Modify the rules of the game

This will frequently lead to greater participation by all team members, and therefore should be beneficial to many. For example:

- no one should travel with the ball;
- no physical contact allowed;
- everyone in the team should touch the ball before an attempt to score is made;
- only certain children can play in certain positions (the disabled child can then choose, or be placed in the safest and most appropriate place).

## Modify the challenges

Reducing the distance to be travelled, allowing a 'runner', lowering the net to make hitting the ball easier, raising it to slow down the flight of the ball, lowering the goal or increasing the target area can all be used to improve participation and increase success.

## Change the activity!

By their very nature, cooperative activities, rather than competitive challenges, require the active involvement of *all* members of the group and are therefore ideal alternatives to the formal team game.

# Subject Specific – Swimming

## Teach how to enter and leave the pool safely

Ideally we are aiming for total independence, but if that is not practicable, then helpers must know how to assist. Invariably it is best if the helper is in the water first, ready to receive the child, and leaves the water last, when the session is finished (see Illustration 8).

## Consider mobility around the pool area

The child who manages to walk wearing supportive shoes may well find walking barefoot on a wet poolside a dangerous challenge. The pool surround must be absolutely safe for the non-ambulant child and every precaution taken to prevent any skin abrasions on insensitive skin which is unprotected. (These can take an inordinately long time to heal because of poor circulation and so mean that swimming is impossible for many weeks.) Remember, also, that the VI child who has left his or her glasses in the changing room might easily become dangerously disorientated by the poolside and in addition could be affected by glare and reflection from the water surface.

## Be alert to the likely effects of the child's disability on his or her natural position in the water

Children who are very overweight, or who have wasted, floppy or paralysed limbs usually float very well. Those with paralysed legs often float with them high in the water, which can be a frightening experience since they feel unbalanced and unable to regain a vertical position. Very muscular or bony children and those who are stiff and experiencing spasm are naturally sinkers for whom floating is difficult. Anyone who is missing a limb, or is paralysed on one side of their body, will have a natural tendency to rotate in the water.

8 Assisted pool entry.

Assisted pool entry, with the child still being in control by initiating the movement.

## Teach how to change position in the water

Because of the points just made, it is extremely important to teach each child how he or she can move from position to position in the water and particularly how he or she can regain a safe, vertical stance, from both a front and a back float. Remember that it is head movement which initiates movement in the rest of the body.

## Do not be too dogmatic over style

Independent and enjoyable movement must be the prime aim, not a perfect swimming style. So many disabilities preclude symmetrical, well coordinated movement that formal stroke technique is unrealistic. However, knowledge of the principles involved in the latter should be related to the child's own efforts, so that these are as efficient and beneficial as possible.

## Choose floatation aids carefully

It may be necessary to have a wider range of aids than usual available, in order to support the child in the desired position. Some aids may restrict already limited arm mobility, whilst others can upset the child's balance in the water or prevent him or her changing positions independently.

## Subject Specific – Gymnastics

### Make large apparatus more accessible

'Access' and 'exit' points may be needed, in order to allow the child to experience working on the main piece of apparatus: inclined forms or stepped boxes can be particularly useful when linked to higher apparatus.

### Make pieces of apparatus wider

Particular skills which the disabled youngster especially needs to practise, such as using different methods of travelling and balancing, may be excluded if the apparatus is too narrow and therefore inappropriately challenging. Two forms or boxes placed side by side could provide the required stable, wide support.

### Encourage varied use of apparatus

Children's natural tendency is to go up and over apparatus. This activity may well be unsafe, unwise or impossible for some individuals.

A more varied use of the apparatus, including going under, around, through and between the elements of it may be just as beneficial, as skills of negotiating around obstacles and appreciating spatial concepts are acquired.

9 Exploration of gym apparatus.

Unconventional but imaginative and challenging exploration of the apparatus.

### Avoid overcrowding

Children with poor balance will be reluctant to try any apparatus work unless they feel they have the space and time they need; others working close by or moving swiftly past could be very off-putting.

### Be alert to demands being made of ambulant children whose mobility is affected

Activities which involve constant stopping and starting, and stopping with control, can be very demanding and extremely hard to achieve. Some practice may help improve performance, but over-use of these skills in group situations could disadvantage less mobile children. Similarly, the need to constantly sit down and listen then stand up to work may prove to be very tiring, and therefore of no real benefit to those children for whom changing position is a real effort. Energy needs to be conserved for the 'content' of the lesson, not used up on its management.

### Encourage taking weight through the shoulder girdles onto flat hands

Many young children with physical disabilities either have poorly developed shoulder and arm muscles, or need to be particularly strong in the arms to

10 Developing shoulder and arm strength.

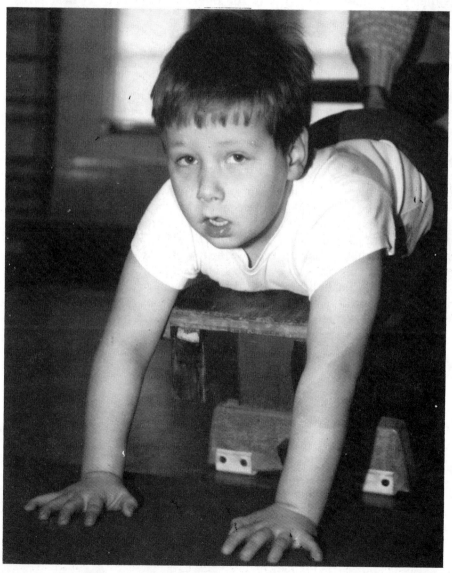

Sliding down off an inclined bench provides an excellent demonstration of weight being taken through straight arms and flat hands – a very beneficial working position.

compensate for paralysed legs. All activities in which weight has to be taken through straight arms onto hands flat on the floor, for example, bunny hops, 'bear' walking and 'wheelbarrows', are highly recommended. It is important to check that the hands are placed down flat with the fingers spread out and the thumb also extended out, not tucked underneath. It is only when the large muscles are developed and the shoulder girdle can be stabilized that the fine control needed for precise hand function can then be fully acquired.

### Remember to allow opportunity for the development of critical skills

The gymnastics lesson provides a wonderful opportunity for the development of particular skills which are crucial to children with certain disabilities. Any who are paraplegic and without the use of their legs, benefit from hanging and swinging activities to develop arm and upper body strength, whilst numerous opportunities for improving balancing skills could naturally occur or be incorporated into lessons for the clumsy and awkward movers.

### Be sensitive as to when support or assistance is needed

In my opinion there is little to be gained from passively lifting a child up onto, or down from the apparatus – a movement in which he or she has taken no part. However, observing when the child begins to take the initiative towards moving onto the apparatus enables you to then provide whatever support or assistance is required for him or her to achieve their goal. For example, it might be necessary to actually place his or her foot on the rung of the climbing frame or to physically help him or her raise their knee high enough to get it up onto a high piece of apparatus. Being sensitive to his or her need and ability should allow sufficient help to be there, without smothering or taking over.

### Know how to support the child correctly

It is often necessary to give a few moments' support to encourage an ambulant child to step up, down, to jump, negotiate obstacles or tackle a balancing task. Holding one hand, which is usually our natural response, tends to put the child into an asymmetrical and off-balance position, which so often we want to avoid. It is far better to assist the child from in front so that you can get eye contact, allowing him or her to hold both your hands, or even better to push down with both his or her hands and straight arms, onto yours. A more confident child could be assisted by steadying him or her from behind with both hands at their hips, so allowing him or her to use their arms freely for balancing.

11 Supporting on gym apparatus.

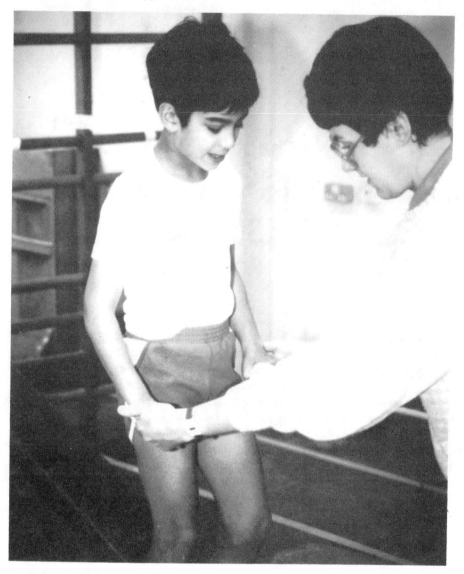

A good position for supporting, which allows the child to retain his symmetry, and adjust the degree of support he needs.

# Chapter 9

# In Conclusion – Illustrative Case Studies

We were introduced to Lisa, David, Steve and Paul at the beginning of this book. Subsequently we have considered both a number of very different disabling conditions, and many varied dimensions of PE teaching, from the points of view of the teacher and the subject. It should now, in conclusion, be helpful to review the situation from the children's angle by discussing these individuals in more detail. This can best be done by considering each as a separate case study, as far as we are able without knowing more details about their own personal school environments. The various management, safety and planning issues, the special considerations for PE, and the possible options to facilitate full and worthwhile participation are now reviewed and summarized in Figures 6 to 9.

Using such a 'case study' approach could prove to be an extremely valuable planning and recording exercise for any individual teacher or team working with a physically disabled child. It can help to focus attention on key issues and implications, as well as stimulating healthy discussion – including the child wherever possible. It should then ensure that the child's PE experiences are as varied and challenging as possible, and of course enjoyable and rewarding too!

As a final reminder and motivator on behalf of Lisa and her friends it is worth noting that in its discussion of the rationale for PE, the NC Working Party (1991, p. 5) states:

> The physical education curriculum should enable all children to benefit. There should be no barriers to access or opportunity based on ability.

> All pupils should recieve a broad and balanced programme of physical education which is differentiated to meet their needs and which coincides with their interests.

**Figure 6** Lisa – a teenager with brittle bones who is constantly wheelchair-bound and often in plaster

| *Special considerations for PE – safety/modifications/'watch-points', etc.* | *Associated planning and organizational issues* | *Possible components of PE programme* |
|---|---|---|
| 1. No 'contact sports' allowed. | 1. Keep Lisa's situation, plus the activities on offer, constantly under review. | 1. Gym and dance alongside peers, either in or out of wheelchair. |
| 2. Aim to achieve as much balance in the programme as possible, working in and out of the wheelchair. | 2. Liaise with parents and therapists. | 2. Swimming. |
| 3. Include swimming – take particular care with pool entry and exit. | 3. Availability of staff or voluntary helper to supervise individual aspects of her programme? | 3. Wheelchair activities, as movement challenge and to develop proficiency. |
| 4. Busy changing rooms may be hazardous. | 4. Include swimming as part of 'contract system' if not available within school. | 4. Individual activities circuit, in 'protected' environment. |
| | | 5. The 'knowledgeable spectator' role, as coach, scorer or umpire. |

D

**Figure 7**  Steve – a spastic hemiplegic lad, with a visual impairment, of junior school age

| Special considerations for PE – safety/modifications/'watch-points', etc. | Associated planning and organizational issues | Possible components of PE programme |
|---|---|---|
| 1. Needs regular exercise, in correct positions and using suitable movement patterns. | 1. Liaise closely with therapists to obtain advice about which activities are recommended and which should be avoided. Liaise with VI teacher to ascertain exact nature of the VI and best teaching strategies. | 1. Swimming – in warm water. |
| 2. Avoid loud noises, excitement or fear. | 2. Aim to incorporate therapy into PE. | 2. Class activities, but modified games lessons, to allow for limitations in ball handling and spatial ability and speed of reaction. |
| 3. Check that glasses are unbreakable so that they can be worn for PE and that the environment is free from hazards. | 3. Allow extra time for changing. | 3. Cooperative games for all. |
| 4. Ascertain whether the wrist splint should be kept on or taken off and whether Steve can manage this himself. | 4. Where and how to include swimming, if not part of school's own programme? | |
| 5. Remember associated problems which may be present, e.g., distractibility; perceptual difficulties. | 5. What colour equipment does Steve see best? | |
| 6. Allow more space and time if working on large apparatus or handling small apparatus. | | |

**Figure 8**  David – a lad of junior school age, with a deteriorating muscle condition necessitating progressive use of a wheelchair

| Special considerations for PE – safety/modifications/'watch-points', etc. | Associated planning and organizational issues | Possible components of PE programme |
|---|---|---|
| 1. No overtiring – allow rest periods intermittently. | 1. Liaise with therapists, ancillary helper and parents. | 1. Swimming – in warm water. |
| 2. Know how to support and lift safely. | 2. Constantly review and amend David's programme so he is realistically challenged but not over-taxed. | 2. Individual wheelchair skills training. |
| 3. Sensitive and enjoyable introduction to wheelchair activities needed. | 3. Allow extra time for changing. | 3. Gym and dance alongside peers. |
| 4. Needs ancillary in support, who is aware of David's condition and the lesson aims. | 4. Where and how to include swimming, if not part of school's programme. | 4. Small group, adapted activities, e.g. seated football, volleyball. |
| 5. Allow more space and time when working on large apparatus. | | 5. Aspects of class games sessions, but with some modification of rules, positioning, equipment. |
| | | 6. Cooperative games for all. |

**Figure 9** Paul – an infant child with spina bifida

| Special considerations for PE – safety/modifi-cations/'watch-points', etc. | Associated planning and organizational issues | Possible components of PE programme |
|---|---|---|
| 1. How is incontinence managed and by whom? | 1. Extra time and privacy needed for toiletting and changing. | 1. Class activities, allowing more time and space on large apparatus. |
| 2. Remember site of shunt will be vulnerable and no forward rolls should be allowed without medical advice. | 2. Liaise with parents re management of incontinence, and with therapists: joint planning with ancillary. | 2. Cooperative activities for all. |
| 3. Protect all bare skin on legs and feet. | | |
| 4. Should orthopaedic boots be taken off? Can Paul manage these himself? | | |
| 5. Remember perceptual and coordination problems may also be present. | | |
| 6. Needs ancillary in support who is aware of Paul's needs and the PE aims. | | |

## Reference

DES and Welsh Office (1991) *Physical Education for Ages 5–16*, Proposals of the Secretary of State for Education and Science and the Secretary of State for Wales, London: HMSO.

# Appendix A:
# Award Schemes

## British Telecom/British Sports Association for the Disabled: 'Water Learning Awards'

These are described as 'the first steps towards confidence in the water for every-one' and are designed as a stepping stone to other awards. Basic skills of pool entry, submerging, recovery, rotation, floating, gliding and swimming, water-manship and pool exit are covered, and achievement can be rewarded at three levels. The child's own PE teacher or swimming teacher is allowed to 'test'. The awards are useful for building confidence, skill and independence in the water and provide a good incentive for further work. Recommended for youngsters being introduced to swimming as a new activity, but ideal, too for older, dis-abled swimmers who need to gain confidence and learn how to manage their bodies in water.

Further details from: BSAD, Hayward House, Barnard Crescent, Aylesbury, Bucks HP21 9PP (Tel. 0296 27889).

## The Royal Life Saving Society: 'Aquapack'

The Aquapack is a 'comprehensive programme of water confidence, safer swimming and rescue skills'. There are two levels of Aquapack, designed to lead candidates progressively towards a high level of swimming, survival and rescue competence. The Aquapack I, consisting of 4 Aquanaut Awards, aims to develop water confidence and simple survival skills alongside basic swimming skills and is well within the reach of beginners or disabled swimmers. The graded challenges are very positive motivators for the mastery of new skills. No formal qualifications are needed for teaching or examining these awards.

Further details from: RLSS UK, Mountbatten House, Studley, Warwickshire B80 7NN (Tel. 052-785 3943).

### The Royal Society for the Prevention of Accidents: 'Wheelchair Proficiency Award Scheme'

An excellent scheme of awards graded at the three levels of bronze, silver and gold, aimed at progressively increasing wheelchair control, independence and safety awareness. Achievement of an award is marked by an attractive badge to be displayed on the wheelchair. Both manual and electric wheelchair users can participate in the scheme, which at bronze and silver levels can be examined by the person who is responsible for training, although the status of the scheme is enhanced if a Road Safety Officer is associated with it.

The Award Scheme has potential as an alternative activity, should aspects of the school's traditional PE programme prove unsuitable.

Further details from: RoSPA, Cannon House, The Priory Queensway, Birmingham B4 6BS (Tel. 021-233 2461).

### 'Ten Step Award Scheme'

The Ten Step Scheme, which includes an integrated scheme devised to encompass children with special needs, aims to develop motor skills in children in the 7 to 10 age-group through enjoyable and 'play-like' activities. Skills of running, throwing and jumping are included, which form the basic elements of athletics, but are also beneficial to development in other sports and activities. Twenty events are included; scores in five are submitted for the award itself. Children are competing only against themselves, to improve their own scores, but in this scheme are encouraged to take part in officiating too, so that they begin to understand fair competition and basic rule-keeping. For children with special needs, both the activities and the scoring tables have been adapted so that each individual is suitably challenged.

Further details from: Ten Step, c/o Paul Burrows, Sycamore Sports Centre, Hungerhill Road, St Ann's, Nottingham NG3 4NB (Tel. 0602 603475).

### The Amateur Athletic Association/Esso: 'Five Star Award Scheme'

This is a carefully structured and graded scheme which has been designed to introduce youngsters to a wide range of athletics events and to encourage them to participate in athletics at their own level. It aims to meet the needs of every individual, whatever their ability, and to improve their performances by competing only against themselves. Special scoring tables are available for athletes with a physical disability, and special provision is also made for the visually impaired. Some specialist events are included for the physically disabled; the majority of events are the same, but scored differently, making these ideal challenges to use in an 'integrated' coaching situation. Performances are judged by the person responsible for athletics in the school, and free certificates are awarded for achievement at any of the five levels; cloth and metal badges can be bought.

Further details from: M. Gallacher, 26 Barfield Crescent, High Ash, Leeds LS17 8RU (Tel. 0532 689043).

# Appendix B: Recommended Reading – An Annotated Bibliography

*The Educational Implications of Disability* (1985) by J. Male and C. Thompson. Published by RADAR, Hertford.

RADAR have prepared a really useful handbook for all teachers in ordinary schools who have disabled children in their classes. It is presented in clear sections, one of which is general and covers various needs which may apply to any child with a disability, the second containing information about specific disabilities, including a description of the disability plus educational implications in terms of learning difficulties and management and organizational issues. References are made to PE too, within the wider educational context, making this a book which has value for subject and general classteachers, alike.

*Special Needs in Ordinary Schools: Children with Physical Disabilities* (1989) by Paula Halliday. Published by Cassell, London.

As well as discussing the most common disabilities in children and the implications for schooling, Halliday presents many of the wider issues regarding integrated education in a thoroughly practical and readable manner. This book, written by an ex-headteacher, is an extremely informative, helpful and wide-ranging overview, and includes sections on preparing for integration, management of mobility and incontinence, communication, social adjustment, sex education and leisure and recreation.

*The Motor Impaired Child* (1990) by Myra Tingle. Published by NFER-Nelson, Windsor.

Although not specifically about PE teaching, this easily readable, comprehensive book deals with many issues surrounding the integration of motor-impaired children into mainstream schools and could provide much useful, general advice for teachers meeting disabled children for the first time. A range of physical disabilities is described, together with the problems posed by limited mobility and the educational implications of motor impairment. A whole section is dedicated to the range of other professionals who may be involved, and to support agencies. This is an excellent book for anyone who wants to fully appreciate the issues involved in integrated education, and what everyday life can be like for the disabled child.

*Physical Education for Children with Special Educational Needs in Mainstream Education* (1989) by the British Association of Advisers and Lecturers in PE. Published by White Line Press, Leeds.

BAALPE have compiled an excellent factual and easily readable book which is also packed with practical suggestions and advice. Thoughts on establishing a school policy and on assessment and record-keeping add to discussions about the role of the teacher and the dimensions of the subject. The needs of the children and their various disabilities, plus the implications for PE are also quite thoroughly reviewed, providing considerable background information for teachers who are new to this field.

*Physical Education for Special Needs* (1979) edited by Lilian Groves. Published by Cambridge University Press, Cambridge.

This serves as a general, introductory text. The editor first cites plenty of evidence to reinforce the view that PE is a vital component in the curriculum for children with special needs, to which are added contributions from a range of specialists in their own fields, so that many of the major skill areas are discussed. Although written pre-Warnock and therefore somewhat light on integration issues, the book nevertheless provides considerable interesting information which could be applied to the mainstream setting.

*Physical Education and the Physically Handicapped Child* (1980) by Robert Price. Published by Lepus Books, London.

Price wrote his book whilst a practising physical educationalist, and draws on a wealth of experience as a PE teacher in a special school in describing how to develop a PE programme for physically handicapped children. This is a most comprehensive text, packed with advice which could be useful to teachers running integrated PE, including details of the major handicapping conditions and movement potential/considerations for PE, associated disorders, and structuring a programme. All the components of PE are reviewed in some detail and numerous practical tips, coaching points, administrative points and safety and medical advice are also provided, making this a reference book to be thoroughly recommended.

*Physical Education for Handicapped Children* (1983) by S. George and B. Hart. Published by Souvenir Press, London.

Although a large section of this book outlines an activities circuit run in one particular special school, parts of it, written jointly by the school's PE teacher and physiotherapist, could be helpful to mainstream teachers, since basic information about different types of disability and about the various components of a PE programme are included, together with certain 'watchpoints', coaching points and teaching progressions.

*Helping Clumsy Children* (1980) edited by N. Gordon and I. McKinlay. Published by Churchill Livingstone, London.

Although written a decade ago, this remains the most comprehensive and helpful text which is generally available. Multidisciplinary contributions provide a wide-ranging review of what is known of the condition, its manifestations and possible effects on different learning processes, including PE, together with different types of intervention and remedial strategies. Case studies and examples of children's work illustrate points made throughout the book, most graphically. Thoroughly recommended.

*The Child with Motor/Learning Difficulties* (1986) produced by the Occupational Therapy Department of the Royal Aberdeen Children's Hospital.

This small booklet provides a valuable discussion, in layman's language, which defines terms, outlines common features, examines components and describes one department's approach to remediation and treatment. Contributions from parents illustrate very clearly the extent of the difficulties experienced by the child and the tensions and frustrations likely to develop in the adults with whom he or she interacts. This booklet is full of general information, advice and useful tips, much of which could help PE teachers in their understanding of these children.

*Graded Activities for Children with Motor Difficulties* (1988) by James Russell. Published by Cambridge University Press, Cambridge.

Russell has written this book primarily for non-specialist PE teachers working in primary schools, who are dealing with children who have a range of motor and learning difficulties. Programmes of graded activities are provided, which could be used on their own or easily incorporated into class PE lessons. A wide range of very useful and imaginative ideas is extremely well presented, with clear explanations, logical progressions and excellent diagrams. As 14 major motor skill or developmental areas are covered, teachers should be able to select appropriate activities for children to allow for their much needed success and improvement.

*Active Games for Children with Movement Problems* (1987) by Alan Brown. Published by Harper and Row, London.

Brown can write from the position of a sportsman, PE teacher and parent of a disabled child, so he has a wealth of experience and knowledge to share. His book is a finely detailed discussion of the acquisition of games skills and the various effects of disability on performance, together with an analysis of teaching basic games skills and developing group activities and major team games. It is intended as a source of material for teachers in special schools, but could be useful for mainstream staff if they have the time to read and absorb all the contents!

*Swimming for the Disabled* (1981) by the Association of Swimming Therapy. Published by E.P. Publishing, Wakefield.

All areas of swimming education are covered, from the theory affecting floatation, buoyancy, rotation, turbulence and propulsion and the various effects of disabilities on a body's activity in the water, to watermanship games, confidence-building activities, safety and running a gala. A detailed book covering quite specific topics in both theoretical and practical ways and therefore useful to anyone wanting to fully understand this area of the PE curriculum and to teach it well.

*The Co-operative Sports and Games Book* (1978) by Terry Orlick. Published by Writers and Readers Publishing Co-op Ltd, London.

Her concern that too many children are left out of or fail in conventional competitive games led Orlick to develop a positive alternative. Her games involve acceptance, consideration and sharing through an atmosphere of cooperative play and are therefore ideal for all children. The book contains an abundance of ideas for activities for children of all ages, using only basic equipment and is an excellent resource for teachers introducing cooperative games.

*Developmental Movement for Children* (1990) by Veronica Sherborne. Published by Cambridge University Press, Cambridge.

For anyone interested in using Sherborne's 'relationship play' approach to movement development this is an excellent book serving both as an explanatory text and resourcebook of activities. Sections on what to teach and why and how to teach it, are complemented by superb photographs which illustrate Sherborne's philosophy most graphically. Numerous examples of suggested activities in the various types of relationships are clearly described, and an observation checklist and developmental summary are also included, making the book useful for teachers of mainstream, special and pre-school children alike.

# Appendix C:
# Useful Addresses

## Relating to disability

The Arthritis and Rheumatism Council
41 Eagle Street
London
WC1R 4AR
(071-405 8572)

Association for Spina Bifida and Hydrocephalus
  (ASBAH)
22 Upper Woburn Place
London
WC1H 0EP
(071-388 1382)

Asthma Society
300 Upper Street
London
N1 2XX
(071-226 2260)

British Deaf Association (BDA)
38 Victoria Place
Carlisle
Cumbria
CA1 1HU
(0228 48844)

British Diabetic Association
10 Queen Anne Street
London
W1M 0BD
(071-323 1531)

British Epilepsy Association
Crowthorne House
New Wokingham Road
Wokingham
Berks
RG11 3AY
(0344 773122)

British Heart Foundation
14 Fitzhardinge Street
London
W1H 4DH
(071-935 0185)

Brittle Bone Society
112 City Road
Dundee
DD2 2PW
(0382 67603)

The Cystic Fibrosis Research Trust
Alexandra House
5 Blyth Road
Bromley
Kent
BR1 3RS
(081-464 7211)

Disabled Living Foundation
380–384 Harrow Road
London
W9 2HU
(071-289 6111)

Friedrich's Ataxia Group
Burleigh Lodge
Knowle Lane
Cranleigh
Surrey
GU6 8RD
(0483 272741)

Muscular Dystrophy Group of Great Britain and
    Northern Ireland
Nattrass House
35 Macaulay Road
London
SW4 0QP
(071-720 8055)

National Children's Bureau (NCB)
8 Wakley Street
London
EC1V 7QE
(071-278 9441)

The National Deaf-Blind and Rubella Association
    (SENSE)
311 Gray's Inn Road
London
WC1X 8PT
(071-278 1005)

Royal Association for Disability and Rehabilitation
    (RADAR)
25 Mortimer Street
London
W1N 8AB
(071-637 5400)

Royal National Institute for the Blind (RNIB)
224 Great Portland Street
London
WC1N 6AA
(071-388 1266)

Royal National Institute for the Deaf (RNID)
105 Gower Street
London
WC1E 6AH
(071-387 8033)

The Spastics Society
12 Park Crescent
London
W1N 4EQ
(071-636 5020)

## Relating to PE

Amateur Swimming Association (ASA)
Harold Fern House
Derby Square
Loughborough
Leics
LE11 0AL
(0509 230431)

Association of Swimming Therapy (AST)
4 Oak Street
Shrewsbury
Shropshire
SY3 7RH
(0743 4393)

British Blind Sport
Dept C
Heygates Lodge
Elkington
Yelvertoft
Northants
NN6 7NH
(0858 575584)

British Sports Association for the Disabled (BSAD)
Hayward House
Barnard Crescent
Aylesbury
Bucks
HP21 9PP
(0296 27889)

CP Sports
Spastics Society
Sycamore Sports Centre
Hungerhill Road
St Ann's
Nottingham
NG3 4NB
(0502 692314)

Duke of Edinburgh's Award Scheme
Award Offices
5 Prince of Wales Terrace
London
W8 5PQ
(071-937 5205)

Physical Education Association of Great Britain and
   Northern Ireland (PEA)
Ling House
5 Western Court
Bromley Street
Digbeth
Birmingham B9 4AN
(021-753 0909)

Physically Handicapped and Able-Bodied Clubs
   (PHAB)
Tavistock House North
Tavistock Square
London
WC1H 9HX
(071-388 1963)

Riding for the Disabled Association (RDA)
Avenue 'R'
National Agriculture Centre
Stoneleigh
Kenilworth
Warwickshire
CV8 2LY
(0203 56107)

# Index